Pot Belly Pig.

Pot Belly Pigs as Pets.

Pot Belly Pig owners guide including care, costs, health, training and grooming.

By

Charlie Hardman

Table of Contents

Introduction

Pigs are very intelligent animals, especially pot belly pigs. These exotic animals are not common when it comes to owning pets, but how can you look away from their adorable eyes and that cute pink nose? Owning a pet is a big decision no matter how easy it may seem.

Attitudes towards pigs have changed during the course of history. In some cultures, they have been worshipped – in others, reviled as disease carriers and rejected by some religions as untouchable. However, pigs are very clean by nature – and it is only humans forcing them into certain conditions on their way to slaughter which gave rise to them being mistakenly seen as filthy. And let's face it, the actual word "pig" has been used as a derogatory term throughout the ages. Conversely, there are many pig lovers out there, charmed by their face and shape who, in the absence of being able to keep one as a pet, satisfy their interest in the purchase of collectibles – ornaments, jewellery, plush toys and so on.

Pot-bellied pigs are usually smaller in size comparatively to other average farm pigs that are found in America as well as in the UK. They have been given their name because of the shape of their bellies. They are also considered the same species as wild boars and farm pigs. Small in stature and able to be trained a domesticated pet, these animals have become extremely popular pets over the years. Most city councils accept them as pets within their areas, provided they have been neutered and vaccinated just like any other domestic pet. But, as with any other pet, committing yourself to owning one is a full-time responsibility and one to be taken very seriously. This book will provide you with the information required on owning one as a pet.
Please note that pot belly pig is the same as a pot-bellied pig and you will find both terms used in this book.

Chapter 1. Pot Belly Pig History and Facts

Pot-bellied pigs have a very interesting and long history. Originating from Asia, these pigs are known popularly to be from their Vietnamese background. Families used to use the pot-bellied pigs as a source of food and fat. Unlike the other farm pigs who have a fat proportion of 5-20%, pot-bellied pigs are 50% fat.

In the past 100 years, the pigs came to Europe. Their breed started to become very popular when, during the midst of the 80s, a man named Connell shipped them off to Canada. There they were used to conduct many experiments due to their efficient size, and they are relatively close to regular farm pigs and hogs.

During the late 80s, Connell pigs were then shipped off to America, where they were displayed in zoos. The zoo owners had them bred and sold their offspring and the breed gained popularity rapidly. The pigs were often sold to farmers and breeders during this time. The farmers and breeders eventually bred the pigs with other bloodlines, creating mixed breeds. These mixed breeds were selected and put through competitions to see which one had created the best one.

The winners of the competition were then sold for a lot of money. During this pink era, the first pot-bellied pig association came forth. The pigs were registered, were researched, and their entire history had been chased all the way back to Vietnam. In fact, some very surprising information that came forth was that pot-bellied pigs are descendants of the Chinese pigs who were domesticated 10,000 years ago!

Unfortunately, these pigs were abandoned after they lost their popular standing. The association also stopped registering the pigs, and they were left alone. With no proper care, food source, and required treatment, the pot-bellied pigs faced severe malnutrition. Thus came the teacups; these are actually the malnutrition breed of the pot belly pigs due to their size and weight, although their organs are completely normal.

As time passed, many people adopted these pigs as farm animals, either for a source of food and fat, to breed for offspring, or to keep them as pets. The pot-bellied pigs became popular as pets, especially the teacups due to their size. They were the same size as farm pigs, and were fun to keep, as they easily got along with others.
As the years continued, more breeders mixed the bloodline of pot-bellied pigs with others. Most of them bred pot-bellied pigs with farm hogs, as they are known to be cousins and are quite similar to each other.

Nowadays, all of the pot-bellied pigs in the United States are known to be mixed breeds and not genuine pot-bellied. The several breeds that were created include the Swedish White, Juliana, KuneKune, Teacup, and the Pot-bellied Hogs.

1) Some Facts about Pigs
The cat meows, the dog barks and the pig oinks. It is the specific noise that they make to interact with their surroundings. If you've ever been to the farmhouse or a place with pigs, you might already be familiar with its sound. The noise is typical of a pig; if you are bothered by it, you might want to reconsider your decision! Apart from that, there are quite a few things about the pig, which makes it a worthy companion. In fact, quite a few people changed their perceptions about a pig after having it as a pet.

Here are some of the facts about keeping pigs as pets that might convince you to try it out. Don't rush yet; there is a lot to be learned before you can actually head out to buy one!

- Pigs Converse! They have a series of oinks, grunts and squeals which signify different emotions.
- Pigs are intelligent. In fact, they are often regarded as more intelligible species compared to children under the age of three, dogs, cats and other animals!
- Contrary to popular belief, pigs are clean animals. They like keeping their sleep area spotless and would usually head out to relieve themselves. They are extremely easy to potty train.
- They are generally social and peaceful creatures. They like mixing with other animals but do particularly well with their own kind. They generally do not get aggressive, though if they are left alone for too long, they might become reserved and unhappy.
- They get affected by the seasons and it shows in their behavior. They tend to be excited and hyped up during the summer season while the winters are slow, depressing and irritable for them. An irresponsive pig especially during the winters is normal
- The Chinese Zodiac has it too. The pig represents happiness, fortune, virility, and honesty.
- The pig is an essential part of the ecological system. They help build new plant colonies and spread seeds and pollen. Their rooting behavior disturbs the soil to provide favorable conditions for new plants to grow.
- Pigs are omnivores. In fact, they would gobble up just about anything you hand out to them. Be mindful of your fingers; you don't want them to be near their food while they are feeding.
- According to their body size, pigs have small lungs. Even the slightest hint of a lung disease can kill it.
- Most pigs that are slain for food are about six months old. This means they are deprived of at least 95% of their lifespan.
- A famous British writer (who also served as the Prime Pot-bellied twice during the 20th century) praised the pig species in the following words, "Dogs look up to Man. Cats look down to Man. Pigs look us straight in the eye and see an equal!"
- Pigs have good memory and sense of direction. They can find their way back home from extremely large distances.

- Like dogs, pigs are known to be saviors. Although this particular aspect about pigs is not popular, there have been instances where a pig helped its master escape accidents.

If you find the idea of keeping a pig as a pet fascinating, the next section will help you to decide whether it would be the right decision for you to have a pet Pot-bellied pig.

2) Should You Consider Getting a Pig as a Pet?

It is almost like asking whether you should get a dog as a pet or not; there is no generalized answer to the question. It all depends on you whether you'd like to take one in or not.

However, there are a few other considerations you will need to take into account before moving forward with your decision.

For the most part, pigs are amiable beings, but in some countries and regions, keeping pigs as pets is not considered legal. For instance, across several regions in Australia, keeping pigs as pets – even in the backyard – is strictly forbidden.

In other areas, you might need special permits in order to walk your pet pig or have it transported to any other place. Make sure you check in with the laws of your region before opting to purchase a pig. If it isn't legal, it will only get you into trouble.

Besides this, there may be other restrictions with respect to their upkeep. For instance, the government might impose certain restrictions about what the pigs are to be fed or what they shouldn't be fed. Moreover, some laws prohibit the burial of a pig. Go through all the rules and regulations pertaining to pigs in your region before you get one.

Another important consideration you need to take into account is this; will you be able to give it the time and affection required to keep it from becoming violent? How will your pig get along with other pets you may have in your home?

A pig that feels neglected may transform into a monstrous creature. It may not be apparent from their innocent faces but they have the capacity to wreak havoc in your house.

If you are too busy to give it time, you can try buying two pigs to keep each other company. If that is too expensive, the next best option is to leave this job to those who are well suited for it!

Do you have the adequate outside space for the pig to exercise and display its natural behavior of grazing and rooting? If you don't, do you have the time to walk and exercise your pig?

Keep in mind that you will need to get your pig tattooed in the ear or add an identification tag to it. It is ordained by law to brand your pig so that it can be identified if and when the need arises. Can you find a veterinarian who is able to take care of the pig's health requirements, vaccinations and deal with any illnesses it may suffer?

Pigs like to snuggle up with their owners, but their rooting instincts cannot be stopped. If you have any reservations about the natural lifestyle of a pig, it is advised for you not to try keeping it as a pet. The pig does not become "cultured" simply because it is being brought up in a home. It will behave more or less the same way as it would on a farm or in the wild.

It will consume anything and everything that is strewn across the floor (or any other place where it can reach) – this includes debris and garbage of all sorts. If this is not the kind of behavior you expect from your pet, it is pointless pursuing keeping a pig as a pet.

The choice is yours to make. If you can keep up with an unconventional pet that has its specific needs, keeping a pig as a pet may be a good idea.

Whether it will do the same for you or not, this depends on your willingness to accommodate a stout little creature in your house and your life.

3) The Questions to Ask Yourself

There are a few questions that you need to ask yourself in order to gauge how serious you are about keeping pigs as pets. Never follow this pattern merely as a trend. Pet pigs are infinitely different from other animals. Make absolutely sure that you are looking for a pet pig before you decide to bring one home. If you can't live with the mess they are known to create, it is best to stay away from the association altogether!

Here is a list that might help you make the right decision. When you've answered these questions, evaluate them with a critical perspective. If, by the end of it, you still feel motivated enough to bring home a pet pig, then by all means you should proceed with the acquisition phase.

1) Do you have the time and resources to care for a pet pig?
2) Do you really want to have a pet pig or are you just looking for a not-so-common pet for a companion? Have you evaluated other alternatives like birds, hamsters, turtles, and others?
3) How much do you know about pigs' needs and breeds?
4) Do you have a lot of distractions that will make it difficult for you to care for a pet pig?
5) Do you travel a lot? If yes, how long do you think you will be away for? Can you take your pet pig on your trips?
6) Do you know how fast specific pig breeds tend to grow and how they will be when they mature?
7) Do you have access to a veterinarian doctor who will take a look at your pet pig if it is ill? It isn't a conventional pet, so you might have trouble finding a doctor to consult if and when your pig gets ill.
8) Can you tolerate their natural habits like rooting? Do you have space in your backyard to accommodate their natural instincts? If these sound too dirty or disgusting, rest assured you won't be able to care for your pet pig in the right manner.
9) Can you keep up with a moody pet? Pigs get affected easily by seasonal changes. They tend to become somber during winter and hyperactive during the summer season.
10) Can you accommodate a pet pig indoors? Pigs aren't outdoor pets, so you'll need to give them a space within your roomy interiors. However, if you can't do so, it will affect your pig's health negatively.

Evaluate the pros and cons of your decisions carefully before you decide to bring a pig home. Once you've adopted it, there is little chance you'll be able to get rid of the association responsibly before a decade or two.

Chapter 2. All About Breeds

Once you've decided on getting a pig as a pet, the next thing you need to figure out is - which one? This section talks about how you should select a pig. It shouldn't be random; you need to know exactly what you are getting yourself into. Read through carefully, it will make a lot of difference to your adventurous journey.

Pot-bellied pigs belong to the family of wild boars and farm pigs. Pot-bellied pigs are known as pot-bellied pigs because of their size. Pot-bellied pigs also include KuneKune pigs, Teacups, and Pot-bellied Hogs.They all are cousins so to speak and look remarkably alike.

Brief Comparisons of the Breeds
Pot-bellied pigs weigh in at a massive 43 to 136 kg. The KuneKune pig, on the other hand, weighs around 400 pounds, which is close enough to the weight of an average farm pig. The Pot Belly hog is different in terms of looks. Unlike the pot-bellied and KuneKune pigs, the hogs are a bit thinner and taller, and can be compared to a large pot in terms of size.

Teacups, or Micro Pot-bellieds, are also pot-bellied pigs. Unfortunately, due to malnutrition and other health concerns, their size and weight is not up to the average Pot Belly pig. However, even though these pigs remain tiny, the size of their organs remains normal.

KuneKune Pigs
KuneKune pigs are actually a line of pot-bellied pigs that have been bred with each other containing different or the same bloodlines. These pigs have been around since the 1900s and were known for their popularity in New Zealand. The name KuneKune means 'round and fat,' just like the pigs. In the midst of the 20th century these pigs became a popular source of pork. Around the 1980s, they almost became extinct; in fact hardly 50 KuneKune pigs were left. This is when farmers resorted to mixed breeding and the KuneKune pigs became a part of a recovery program, which began in New Zealand to save the breed.

KuneKunes are really easy to spot. This breed of pot-bellied pigs is hairy, comes in different colors, and is covered in spots. Their hair color even varies, with pink, ginger, cream, gold, white, tan, and black. Another way in which you can easily identify them is by their lower jaw. KuneKunes have tassel jaws, which means their lower jaw has piri piri under its chin. The pigs are short, round, as their name says, and have small legs. Their average height is of 60 cm.

Vietnamese Pot-bellied pig

Many of these pigs have been abandoned by their owners because their pig was growing a lot larger than they expected. Because the body of a Vietnamese Pot Belly pig is very solid and compact, these pigs can weigh up to 200 pounds without being overweight. The average weight is between 120 and 140 pounds.

Teacups

Teacup pigs are the offspring of four of the main pig breeds, one of which is pot-bellied pigs. The mixed bloodline of the pot-bellied and other breeds such as the KuneKune resulted in the teacup. Due to genetics, the pigs are small, which is why they are also known as micro pigs. Fake breeders or owners who lack information about teacups will assure you that they remain the same size throughout their lifespan, which is not true. Teacups can grow, and they do not remain the same size all their lives. If a breeder or an owner tells you this, there are two reasons behind it: either they have starved the pigs, or they are themselves unaware regarding the breed.

Teacup Appearance

Teacup pigs are really adorable. They are small in size but can eventually grow up to 15 inches; some even grow to be larger than that as well. The teacups weigh less than 55 pounds, but their weight can exceed this as well. Commonly kept as pets, there is no breed that has been properly established under their name. The pigs vary in color depending on the parents or the owners, can have spots, are small in size, and are fun to play with.

Chapter 3. Where to Buy a Pot-bellied Pig

1) Establishing a Genuine Source

Like every other animal you would like to take in as a pet, you need to be careful about where you purchase your pet pig. Establishing a genuine breeder should be one of your topmost concerns if you are hoping to have a long and healthy relationship with your pet. Do your research carefully! Internet searches will show lists of breeders and from there you can enquire online or make a call – and most importantly, arrange a visit to see the animals. Some local pet and animal feed stores (especially pet stores that sell these animals) will be able to supply you with these animals or put you in contact with the breeders themselves.

Locating genuine and responsible breeders takes time and research. Even then, this does not necessarily mean that you will be able to find the breed of choice. You need to be patient and consistent with your efforts in finding a breeder.

Keep in mind that the way your pet pig turns out depends largely on the breeder. The general rule of thumb is that a litter produced using healthy pigs will have a longer lifespan and be less prone to medical problems. In contrast, cross breeding or producing litter using diseased parents will result in the contrary. A breeder therefore is in control of the situation and needs to have ethical practices in order to promote longevity and healthy pigs.

Make sure you ask the breeder as many questions as you like, even to the point of irritating the breeder. This ensures you are able to get the best deal. Put all your concerns to rest before you walk away with your pot-bellied pig in your hands. The trickier part tends to be locating possible breeders within your vicinity. Given the nature of pig breeding in certain parts of the world, it might prove to be challenging just to locate a pig breeder, let alone a genuine or responsible one. So here are a few tips you can use on your hunt for pig breeders.

Firstly, look for links through the local pig clubs and associations. They will help you get in touch with the closest breeder. Because of their strict qualifying procedures, you can rest assured that the links will be authentic and the breeders you get in touch with will be responsible. However, generally, such associations will not have an exhaustive network of pig breeders. If you are unable to get the contacts you are looking for, you'll need to find your own contacts.

Search for pig breeders online. Try to locate livestock farming units within your vicinity that participate in pig rearing. Farms are a good place to purchase a pig from given you've ensured their breeding practices are in line with those set by local laws and pig breeding associations. Make sure you visit them personally before having your pet shipped to your house. Better still, pick your pet from the farm yourself so you have a better idea of what it is accustomed to. This will help significantly down the line when you are helping your pet pig settle in to your house.

If there is anyone you know who has acquired a pet pig, s/he will have a valuable lead for you to pursue. Get the details of the breeder and conduct your research to ensure it is a responsible one. In addition, keep an eye on the development of this pig to see if it is prone to health problems or not.

Lastly, if you still haven't had much luck trying to locate the pig breeder, you can try searching local pet shops for some information. Although it is not recommended for you to purchase your pet pig from these shops – primarily because they don't share the intricate details about the parents and homing – it will nevertheless help you get started with your hunt.

Ask the pet shop owners about where they acquire their animals from and how they ensure the breeds are pedigree. Look for open and satisfactory answers. If they are not sharing important information about the pet acquiring process, it is better to look elsewhere. It is better not to have a pet than to settle for one which is prone to a number of behavioral and health problems.

Establishing a genuine source is therefore integral to a long-term association with your pet. This is probably the longest part of your pet hunt. Make sure you read about the local rules and regulations pertaining to pet pigs as well. It is not always easy to keep a pig as a pet, especially where legal rules are extremely restrictive. Make sure you ask the breeders for their registration papers with the local pig clubs. If they are unable to provide these, the next best thing you can ask for are medical certificates of both the parents used for the litter. Pig breeding is an age-old practice but it has conventionally focused on different reasons. As pet owners, you don't want a breed that accumulates more muscle and doesn't live beyond the first year! Choose the breeder wisely; it will help you a lot during the course of your companionship.

2) Meeting its Parents

Another important aspect of the pet acquiring process is meeting the litter's parents. Most genuine breeders will have them on the breeding grounds. Even if they don't, make sure you ask them for pictures just to be sure that they are fit and healthy.

Pictures of the extended family are to be considered as a bonus because these aren't necessary. However, you need to ask as much as possible about the parents. This is because genetics tend to replicate within the litter seamlessly, so even if the litter looks perfectly healthy during the initial months, they will be at risk of developing several health problems during the latter years if the parents had the same tendency.

Besides having a look at the parents, make sure you ask the breeder for their medical certificates as well. These documents declare the species clear of all major health problems and hence fit for mating. The absence of these records points towards an uncertainty with respect to your pet pig's health.

Another important thing that you need to verify is this; what was the age of the parents when they were allowed to mate? If the parents were too young – that is, within the first two years of their lives – then most genetic problems will not have surfaced by the time they were allowed to mate. In essence, medical certificates of pigs below two years of age do not have authenticity or value with respect to ethical breeding practices.

The first value lessons learnt by the litter are from their parents. Make sure you don't separate them before this value transmission is complete. This phase helps the pigs learn their characteristic habits (like rooting).

Cross breeding in pigs is not really considered as an illegal activity, but when this happens, you need to be extra careful about adopting the littermates. While cross breeding practices are adopted to improve the quality and life of a pig, most end up in disaster. Especially if you are new to the task of keeping pigs as pets, it is recommended for you to pursue pedigree breeds only.

3) The Questions to Ask the Breeder
If this is your first ever pet pig purchase and you have no one to guide you to a reputable breeder, you'll need to figure out the genuineness of the breeder by asking specific questions.

While at it, keep in mind that you have every right to get to know the breeder as well as the litter before you put down the payment, even if the breeder gets irritated by the questions.

A genuine and ethical breeder will never refrain from addressing your concerns. In fact, the authentic ones will ask you a couple of questions too in order to make sure you are the right owner for the pig!

Here's what you should definitely ask your breeder in order to identify how ethical s/he is in the breeding process:
▪ How long have you been in the pig breeding business? The longer, the better.
▪ How many generations of this particular breed have you witnessed? Are there any genetic complications I need to be worried about?
▪ How frequently is a litter expected?
▪ How are the littermates being housed? How are they cared for?
▪ Were the parents certified to be healthy before they were allowed to mate?
▪ What are the terms and conditions of the contract? What guarantees are present?
▪ Are there any other clients you will be allowed to get in touch with in order to understand how the litter grows up to be?

- How to take care of this breed? What to expect from pigs belonging to this breed?
- How is the pig trained and socialized? Has the pig been taken to a veterinary doctor?
- What should I keep in mind while caring for this particular pig breed?

If there are any other questions on your mind, make sure you ask these. Clarifying your doubts need to be one of your top-most priorities.

If you feel the breeder has not been completely honest with you or if there are certain questions the breeder has tried to avoid, you might want to consider looking elsewhere. If you are looking for a healthy relationship with your pet, you would be better off purchasing your pig from a breeder who is willing to share information with you. In fact, professional breeders often look to these questions as a sign of genuine interest. They encourage you to ask questions, as it shows your eagerness to be the best owner for your pet.

4) The Questions to Expect From the Breeder

While you go about your routine trying to establish whether the breeder is authentic and ethical or not, the breeder will also want to make sure you are the right owner for their animals. You can wholly expect them to ask personal questions. They will try to evaluate your resources and availability to keep a pig as a pet. The professional breeders are in no hurry to get their animals adopted, and they'll wait long enough for the right owner to find them. They'll be interested in your lifestyle to see whether there is space to accommodate a pet or not. This helps them ascertain that the pig will be well cared for and will therefore not end up on the street, euthanized, or be brought back to the breeder.

Here are just some of the questions you should expect them to ask:
- What do you do for a living? This not only tells them how much spare time you have to care for your pet, but also illustrates your financial situation.
- Why do you want to keep pigs as pets? Do you have prior experience in caring for pet pigs?
- Where do you live?

- Have you researched about keeping pigs as pets? What do you know about the breed and its needs?
- Do you have any idea how much it costs to care for a pet pig?
If the breeder decides not to give you a pig, you shouldn't despair. Instead, try to understand that the breeder has the best interests at heart, both for the pig as well as for you.

The questions here aim to give you an idea about how you should analyze your needs for a pet. You should not fake answers just to have your way. Instead, be absolutely honest with the breeder; you might be able to find out a few facts you weren't considering before now. It can actually save you from a troubled relationship.

5) Picking The Right One From The Litter

If things go well during the question and answer session, the breeder will introduce you to the pigs available on the farm at that moment. This is where you are required to select your companion. Pigs, especially the younger ones, are absolutely adorable. Their little pink bodies and mischievous behavior will undoubtedly make you want to adopt them all.

However, it is generally a good idea to start with one pig to figure out if it is the right pet for you. Once you've understood your pet's needs, you can move forward with the second, third and the forth as you like.

Selecting a pig from the litter may prove to be a challenging task. A word of advice: don't make your choice simply based on how they look. You need to observe their behavior in order to make the right selection. Their behavior, even when they are little piglets, says a lot about what they will grow up to be.

Here are some pointers that will help you make the right choice:
1). Look for a pig that likes being in the group. The one who lurks away in the corner while the others are playing is most likely to have certain personality disorders. The pig is unsocial from birth; it will take excessive training to make this particular pig social. In contrast to this, a pig that likes being in the crowd will most readily settle in with your lifestyle and will be happy around other pets!

2). A healthy pig will be active and playful. If there is any particular piglet in the litter that seems to be having some problems keeping up with the others, it is likely to develop more health problems in the near future. In fact, if this is the case, we would recommend you not to purchase any piglet from the litter. This is a sure sign of trouble.

3). You definitely want to stay away from aggressive pigs. If any particular pig in the litter seems to be shoving others away without reason, this is the one you should avoid. They can not only cause significant damage to your property and possessions but also pose a significant threat to people. Excessively timid pigs are to be looked at critically as well. Pick a pig that seems to be moderate.

4). Check for obvious signs of health issues. Their coats should be healthy and lively, their eyes should be bright and free from unexplained discharges, and there shouldn't be any stiffness or lameness in the way they walk. A healthy pig will be lively and interactive. They are fun and will therefore serve the purpose of a pet.

5). Interact with it. Put your hand inside the playpen or roam around with them inside it and give the pot belly pigs time to sniff and explore you before you interact with them. Pet the pot-bellied pigs and encourage them to play with you, taking the opportunity to observe their personalities. Then you can single out any of the pot-bellied pigs that you think might be a good fit and spend a little more time with them. You can also pick up the pot-bellied pigs and hold him to see how he responds to human contact. The pot-bellied pigs might squirm a little but it shouldn't be frightened of you and it should enjoy being held.

6). Examine the pot belly pigs' body for signs of any illness and potential injury. The pot belly pigs should have clear, bright eyes with no discharge. Their ears should be clean and clear with no discharge or inflammation. The pot-bellied pigs' body should be rounded without protruding bones. The pot-bellied pigs should be able to walk and run normally without any mobility problems. Keep your requirements in mind while picking a pig from the litter. For the most part, you'll be looking for a well-behaved animal that will accompany you through the years without burdening you.

6) List of Breeders and Rescue Websites

If you want a piglet or a baby pot-bellied pig, you can probably find some at rescue websites. You may also try adopting a pot-bellied pig from a reputable breeder as well, who knows it might be the better option for you. There are plenty of pot-bellied pigs out there that have been abandoned by their previous owners and they are looking for a new forever home. When you adopt a pig, you are actually saving a life, and there are some benefits for you as well.

Adopting a pot-bellied pig can sometimes be cheaper than buying from a breeder. Many pot-bellied pigs are ready for adoption and usually they have also already been spayed or neutered, litter trained, and could also be caught up on vaccinations.

Here is the list of breeders and adoption rescue websites around the United States and the United Kingdom:

Please note that we are unable to verify or recommend breeders in this book and merely refer to them as a source of information for you.

United States Breeders and Rescue Websites

American Pot-bellied Pig Association
www.americanpot-belliedpigassociation.com
Pixie Pigs
www.pixiepigs.com
Texas Tiny Pigs
www.texastinypigs.com
When Pigs Fly Naked
www.whenpigsflynaked.com
Charming Pot-bellied Pigs
www.charmingpot-belliedpigs.com
Sandy Creek Pot-bellied Pigs
www.sandycreekpot-belliedpigs.com
Juliana Pig Asso**ciation
www.julianapig.com
Piggly Wiggly Pot-bellied Pigs
www.pigglywigglypot-belliedpigs.com
Teacup Pigs
www.teacuppigs.info
Pot-bellied Pig Ranch
www.pot-belliedpigranch.com

Teacup Pot-bellied Pigs
www.teacuppot-belliedpigs.com
Teacup Piggies
www.teacuppiggies.com

United Kingdom Breeders and Rescue Websites
Penny Well Farm
www.pennywellfarm.co.uk
Pet Piggies UK
www.petpiggies.co.uk
Courtney's Pet Pigs
www.courtneyspetpigs.co.uk
Kew Little Pigs
www.kewlittlepigs.com
Valley of the Pigs UK
www.valleyofthepigs.co.uk
Micro – Pigs UK
www.micro-pigs.net
Lancashire Micro Pigs UK
www.lancashiremicropigs.co.uk
RSPCA Organization
www.rspca.org.uk

7) Legal Requirements

If you are planning to acquire a pot-bellied pig as your pet, there are certain restrictions and regulations that you need to be aware of. Legal requirements for pot-bellied pigs may vary in different countries, regions, and states.

Here are some things you need to know regarding the acquirement of Pot-bellied pigs both in the United States and the United Kingdom:

United States Licensing for Pot-bellied Pigs
Before you bring home a new pet, it is always a good idea to determine whether there are any laws in your area that require you to register or license your pet.

In the United States, pot belly pigs are under the regulation of the USDA and several city governments. It is highly advisable that you check in first with your local government or ask authorities in your area about the rules before taking your pot belly pig home. There are certain zoning requirements that you may need to abide by depending on which state or city you live in. The reason for this is that many cities do not allow pigs as pets, while in some cities there is a limit as to how many pot belly pigs you can keep.

It is highly recommended that you contact your city government offices to know the requirements but most likely it will fall under the city's livestock regulation.

Once you have read or learned about your city's zoning ordinance with regards to pot-bellied pig restrictions or rules, you can apply or submit important documents or even file an official request regarding keeping your pot-bellied pigs as pets. Make sure that you already own a pet pig, preferably spayed or neutered and in great condition. You also want to make sure that these pigs are housed properly and are under your supervision when walking it outside.

Once you think you are prepared to make your case, you can then contact and set up a meeting with your city council or simply submit your proposal. Of course, the procedures and the offices that will handle your concern may vary from one city to another. Your proposal or request to keep your pot-bellied pig as a pet is not guaranteed to be granted.

United Kingdom Licensing for Pot-bellied Pigs
The licensing rules are quite different in the United Kingdom and in many cases possibly much easier. The information below is applicable in England and Scotland only.

In the UK you need to register your pot-bellied pig first if you want to keep them. You can register as a pig keeper by getting a County Parish Holding (CPH) number from the RPA or the Rural Payments Agency. It is also imperative to tell the Animal and Plant Health Agency (APHA) that you are keeping pigs as pets within the span of at least 30 days after acquiring your pot-bellied pig. The Animal and Plant Health Agency will give you a herd mark, which is 1 or 2 letters with 4 digits, sort of like a code. This will serve as your pot-bellied pigs' identification whenever you travel with it or take it for a walk outside. However, before taking your pot belly pig for a walk you should first get a license at the APHA and give them your route. The agency may not approve your walking route if it passes near a livestock market, a fast food restaurant, or a pig farm because it might pose a health risk. You must also renew your license annually so that you can freely take your pot-bellied pig out for a walk.

Chapter 4. Cost of Care

Owning a pot-bellied pig doesn't come cheap. The fact is that these pigs require maintenance, which means that you have to provide supplies and be able to cover the expenses in order to maintain a healthy lifestyle and environment for your pet. These things will definitely add up to your daily budget, and the cost will vary depending on where you purchase it, the brand of the accessories, the nutrients included in its food, etc. If you want to seriously own a pot-bellied pig as a pet you should be able to cover the necessary costs it entails.

In this section you will receive an overview of the expenses associated with purchasing and keeping a pot belly pig such as food and treats, grooming and cleaning supplies, toys, and regular veterinary care. You will receive an overview of these costs as well as an estimate for each in the following pages of this section.

1) Initial Costs
The initial costs for keeping a pot-bellied pig include those costs that you must cover before you can bring your pig home. Some of the initial costs you will need to cover include your crate and playpen, food and water equipment, supplies and accessories, initial vaccinations, spay/neuter surgery and veterinary exams not to mention the cost of the pot-bellied pig itself. You will find an overview of each of these costs as well as an estimate for each below:

Purchase Price: $600 or £480
The cost to purchase a pot-bellied pig can vary greatly depending on the breed, where you buy him and whether it was pedigreed or not. You can probably find a backyard breeder offering $500 or £480or below, but you cannot be sure of the breeding quality for these pigs. Generally speaking, pet-quality pot-bellied pigs sell for $600 or £480 to as much as $5,000 or £4000 maybe even more depending on the breeder as well.

Crate, Playpen or Baby Gate: average of $100 or £80

Whether you live in a small apartment or have a large space in your backyard, you should definitely purchase a crate where your pot-bellied pig can stay and sleep in as well as a playpen or a baby gate to keep them safe and supervised as well as give them the freedom to move around. Crates and playpens have different sizes, on average it may cost about $100 or £80 but could vary depending on the brand and quality.

Food and Water Bowls: average of $30 or £24

In addition to providing your pot belly pigs with a cage or playpen, you should also make sure he has a set of high-quality food bowls and water bowls. The best material for food bowls is stainless steel because it is easy to clean and doesn't harbor bacteria. Ceramic is another good option. The average cost for a quality stainless steel bowl and water bowl for pigs is about $30 or £24. Depending on the brand, some equipment could cost more than average.

Initial Vaccinations: $50 or £40

Pot belly pigs may require a couple of vaccinations, especially during young age. Your veterinarian can tell you if your pot-bellied pig needs any other vaccinations. To cover the cost of these vaccinations you should budget about $50 or £40 or more just to be prepared.

Spay/Neuter Surgery: $250 or £200

If you don't plan to breed your pot-bellied pig you should seriously consider having him or her neutered or spayed. Unfortunately, the cost to spay or neuter a pig breed is fairly high – around $250 or £200. However, if you keep two pot-bellied pigs of the same sex together, it may not be necessary, unless the rule in your city ordinance may require it.

Supplies/Accessories: average of $30 or £24

In addition to purchasing your pot-bellied pig's crate and other accessories, you should also purchase some basic grooming supplies like nail clippers for its hooves, bathing and cleaning supplies for its tusks and teeth as well as harness or a leash. You may also want to buy baby wipes for sanitary purposes. The cost for these items will vary depending on the quality and also quantity, so you should budget about $30 or £24 or more for these extra costs.

Veterinary Exams: average of $600 or £480 (annually)
In order to keep your pot-bellied pig healthy you should take him to the veterinarian at least once a year. The average cost for an annual vet visit for a pot belly pig is about $600 or £480 or more, not to mention other medical costs that may come up if your pet gets sick.

Needs	Costs
Purchase Price	($490.19 or £390)
Crate/Playpen	($81.70 or £65)
Food/Water Equipment	($24.51 or £18)
Vaccinations	($40.85 or £32)
Spay/Neuter	($204.25 or £161)
Supplies/Accessories	($24.51 or £18)
Total	($866.01 or £680)

*Costs may vary depending on location
**Costs may change based on the currency exchange

2) Monthly Costs
The monthly costs for keeping a pot-bellied pig as a pet include those costs that recur on a monthly basis. The most important monthly cost for keeping a pot-bellied pig is, of course, food. In addition to food, however, you'll also need to think about things like bedding, litter, and veterinary exams. Here is the overview of each of these costs as well as an estimate for each need.

Food Pellets and Treats: $20 or £16
Feeding your pot-bellied pig a healthy diet is very important for his health and wellness. Later on in this book, you will learn how much your pot-bellied pig should eat and the kinds of food you can buy for him. Pot-bellied pig feed and treats need to be replenished every month, that's why you should budget about $20 or £16 per month for food. Pot-bellied pigs also eat wheat and tasty treats depending on your pig's appetite and size. You should also provide your pig with vegetables, which can cost an extra $10 or £8 a month or so.

Bedding and Litter or Potty Pads: around $50 or £40
You may need to buy bedding for your pot-bellied pig as well as some blankets to keep them warm at night. Even if you don't use bedding in the whole cage, you should still provide some kind of hideaway lined with comfy bedding for your pot-bellied pig to sleep in.

It is also recommended that you replace your pig's litter or potty pads once in a while. You should plan to spend about $50 or £40 a month on bedding and litter or potty pads for your pot-bellied pig.

Other Costs: around $15 or £12
In addition to the monthly costs for your pig's food, bedding, and litter, there are also some other cost you might have to pay occasionally. These costs might include things like cleaning or

bathing products or repairs for the playpen. You should budget about $15 or £12 per month for extra costs just to be sure.

Needs	Costs
Food Pellet and Treats	($16.34 - or £12)
Bedding/Litter	($40.85 or £32)
Other Costs	($12.25 or £8)
Total	($69.44 - or £56)

*Costs may vary depending on location
**Costs may change based on the currency exchange

3) Pros and Cons of Pot-bellied Pigs

Now you know the basic information about these pigs as pets, you should take the time to learn the pros and cons of the breed before we go on to more specific details. Every pot-bellied pig breed is different so you need to think about the details to determine whether a pot-bellied pig is actually the right pet for you.

In this section you will find a list of pros and cons for pot-bellied pig breeds:

Pros of Pot-bellied pigs

▪ Pot-bellied pigs come in a variety of colors and patterns depending on the breed, which allows you to choose the best option.
▪ They are intelligent yet emotional and sensitive.
▪ They are active outdoors but can be controlled indoors.
▪ They are hypoallergenic because instead of fur they have hair.
▪ Pot belly pigs are easily trained to use a litter pan which makes it easy to clean up after them.
▪ Generally a friendly, docile pet as long as there is proper introduction or socialization at a young age.
▪ Pot-bellied pigs are easy to care for in terms of their diet. They eat mainly pellets, wheat, and fresh veggies.
▪ Pot-bellied pigs do not require regular grooming and it can be done at home.
▪ Pot-bellied pigs are also trainable.

Cons of Pot-bellied pigs

- Pot-bellied pigs can be quite hard to register for licenses.
- Pot-bellied pigs are cute but it can be a high maintenance pet, especially in terms of needs.
- Generally a good pet but some pot belly pig breeds may not be advisable for very small living spaces and may be restricted in places such as condos and apartments.
- They are prone to depression if left alone for a long time.
- May not be a good choice for a household that already has other pets, unless it is properly socialized.
- Generally not recommended for very young children who don't know how to handle or have never encountered a pot-bellied pig.
- Can be a long-term commitment – most pigs live anywhere from 12 to 18 years or more.
- Cost for maintenance will definitely be an additional expense.
- They are quite smelly and can also get messy around the house or backyard if not properly supervised.
- They are highly motivated by food and can snoop around your kitchen, refrigerators, cabinets or trashcans.

Chapter 4. Meeting Your Pot-bellied Pigs' Nutritional Needs

Feeding your pot-bellied pig is not that complicated. However, its breed type should be taken into consideration to meet its nutritional diet. Pot-bellied pigs, like many other pets, should be given the right amount of recommended food for a balanced nutrition because proper diet can lengthen the life expectancy of your pot-bellied pig. In this section, you'll learn about your pet's nutritional needs as well as feeding tips and foods that are good and harmful.

The entirety of a pigs' diet should be made up of plant products as well as the right amount of pellet foods. It is also important to realize that pigs love to eat a lot, so as an owner you should make sure that your pig's nutritional needs are met. And be careful – that your pig's enthusiasm for gobbling up a meal does not encourage you to overfeed your pig! Overfeeding leads to obesity in your pet, which can cause joint, foot, leg and other health problems that can in fact shorten its lifespan.

It is actually quite simple – a balanced diet for pigs should be made up of high-quality commercial pellets/feeds, hays, fruits, and fresh vegetables. Your pig also needs constant access to fresh water because this too plays a role in your pig's digestion. A pig will drink between 7% and 20% of its body weight in water every single day and of course the amount will vary according to temperature and humidity, activity levels, age and health of the pig and other factors. Just ensure that your pig has easy access to a clean and plentiful supply of water to ensure healthy fluid intake. Below are the kinds of food you should feed your pig.

1) Commercial Pellets
When choosing high-quality commercial pellets/feed to use as your pig's staple diet, it is highly recommended that you buy something from known reputable brands such as Purina or Mazuri. If you want to know the specific grams or cups to feed for your pot-bellied pig, it is better to consult your vet or ask the breeder from whom you purchase the pig so that there would be consistency on the kind of food your pot-bellied pig eats. The amount of food highly depends

on the weight and breeding of your pot-bellied pig, which we will discuss later.

2) Grass Hays/ Grains
Aside from choosing a quality pellet for your pot-bellied pig, you should also stock up on fresh grass hay and wheat grains. Just make sure that the supply of grass your pig is grazing on is chemical-free. Grass hay is loaded with calcium, vitamin A, vitamin D, and other nutrients. The process of eating hay helps to keep your pig's digestive tract healthy and also makes your pig comfortable. Like the pellets, you want to make sure that your hay stays fresh.

3) Fresh Fruit
In addition to fresh hay, you can also feed your pig small amounts of fresh fruit. It is also best to consult your vet on the amount of fruit you can give to your pot-bellied pig. Usually fruits only serve as treats for your pig.

Below are the lists of fruits that are safe for pot-bellied pigs:

Apples (no seeds)
Bananas
Melon
Blackberries
Blueberries
Boysenberries
Breadfruit
Gooseberries
Cantaloupe
Coconut
Cranberries
Durian
Figs
Grapefruit
Honeydew Melon
Jackfruit
Lemons
Lychee
Mango
Orange

Papaya
Pear
Passion fruit
Pineapple
Plums
Strawberry
Star Fruit
Peach (no pits)
Apricot (no pits)
Cherry (no pits)
Tangerines
Watermelon
Nectarines (no pits)
Cherries

4) Fresh Vegetables

Last but definitely not least is fresh vegetables. Just like fruits, fresh veggies also serve as treats during training and use as positive reinforcement. Although commercial pellets comprise most of their diet, vegetables should still be included in your pot-bellied pigs' daily diet.

Here is a list of leafy green vegetables that are safe for pot-bellied pigs:

Acorn Squash
Artichoke
Asparagus
Banana Squash
Bamboo shoots
Beets
Bell Peppers
Black olives
Black Radish
Broccoli
Cabbage
Carrots
Cauliflower
Celery Root
Celery

Cherry Tomatoes
Chives
Corn
Cucumbers
Dandelion
Eggplant
Galangal Root
Green Beans
Green leaf lettuce
Edamame
Lettuce
Lettuce
Mushrooms
Mustard Greens
Okra
Olives
Parsnips
Peanuts (unsalted)
Rhubarb stem/stalk
Snow Peas
Spinach
Spring Baby Lettuce
Sugar Snap Peas
Sweet Potatoes
Swiss chard
Tomatoes
Turnip greens
Turnips
Wasabi Root
Watercress
Winged Beans
Winter Squash
Yellow Squash
Yucca Root
Zucchini

5) Toxic Foods to Avoid

It might be tempting to give in to your pot belly pig when he is at the table, but certain "people foods" can actually be toxic for your pet. As a general rule, you should never feed your pot-bellied pig anything unless you are 100% sure that it is safe.

In this section you will find a list of foods that can be toxic to pot-bellied pigs and should therefore be avoided:

Salt
Plum – Leaves & seeds
Broccoli – Roots & seeds
Cabbage – Roots & seeds
Mustard – Roots & seeds
Lychee – seeds
Rambutan – raw seeds
Longan – seeds
Taro – raw
Cassava roots and leaves
Almond – Leaves & seeds
Acorns & oak leaves
Moldy walnut shells
Elderberries, red berries
Lima beans, raw
Nectarine – Leaves & seeds
Cherry – Leaves & seeds
Tomato leaves and vine
Avocado – Skin and pit
Corn stalks (high in nitrates)
Rhubarb – Leaves (stalk is safe to eat)
Kidney beans, raw
Decayed sweet potatoes (black parts)
Castor beans
Potato leaves and green parts of potato
Apple – Leaves & seeds
Apricot – Leaves & seeds
Pear – Leaves & seeds
Peach – Leaves & seeds
Tobacco – leaves
Nutmeg – in large quantities

6) Healthy Treats

Every time your pet pig follows your command or does something good, you should reward him or her with some healthy treats and snacks. This is also part of positive reinforcement.

Here are some snacks you can feed your pot-bellied pig:

Fruit Chips – Bananas, Apples
Coconut Oil
Coconut Water
Cottage Cheese
Yogurt, Plain or Greek
100% Pumpkin Canned
Fruit Juice with no added sugar
Gerber Toddler Puffs
Applesauce, no sugar added
Baby Food with no added sugar or salt
Baked cookies or muffins
Popcorn Air Popped
Scrambled or hardboiled eggs
Warmed/cooked oatmeal
Whole eggs raw
Whole Pumpkin
Granola
Peanut Butter on celery

7) Tips for Feeding Pot-bellied Pigs

Now that you know what to feed your pot belly pig, you may be wondering what amount or how much to feed him. To make sure that your pot-bellied pig gets the nutrients he needs, you need to adjust his diet based on his weight. Veterinarians and researchers agree that a pot-bellied pig's proper diet should be 2% of its overall body weight. According to other sources it can go as low as 1% and as much as 3% for pot-bellied pigs who are parenting. Also, take into account factors such as your pig's metabolic rate, how old your pig is, how active your pig is and how much exercise it gets.

Obesity is the leading health problem for pigs in general because they love to eat. Do not over feed them or underfeed them, because they will both result to your pot-bellied pigs craving for more.

Chapter 5. Habitat Requirements

The pot-bellied pig makes a wonderful pet largely because of his energetic yet docile personality, but these pigs may or may not be adaptable to different types of living situations. In this chapter you will learn the basics about your pot-bellied pig habitat requirements including the recommended cage type, useful accessories, and exercise requirements. You will also receive other general tips for training and handling your pot-bellied pig.

Unlike other pets, pot-bellied pigs need space to roam around in. They are quite high maintenance because of their size, especially when they become adults, even if they are considered pot-bellied. Aside from space, the main thing your pet pig needs in terms of its habitat is lots of love and affection from his human companions and adequate exercise. Pot belly pigs bond closely with family, so you should make an effort to spend some quality time with your pot-bellied pig each and every day. If your pet doesn't get enough attention he may be more likely to develop behavioral problems, suffer from depression which can lead to potential aggression as well as separation anxiety.

In addition to playing with your pot-bellied pig and spending time with him every day, you also need to make sure that his needs for exercise are met. Pot belly pigs or pigs in general are the fifth most intelligent animal in the world, that's why it's important for you to also make sure your pet gets plenty of mental stimulation during the day. Keep reading to learn the basics about your pig's habitat requirements. You will also learn about recommended crate or kennel accessories and receive tips for choosing the right bedding for your pig as well as some guidelines on how to handle and train your pet.

1) Ideal Habitat for Pot-bellied Pigs
You can either put your pot-bellied pig in a kennel crate or set up a playpen around your house or backyard. Follow the guidelines below to ensure that your pet is comfortable.

Crate or Kennel

You can buy a 700 Series Veri Kennel that is preferably large or at least twice the size of your pigs. As an alternative, you can build a three-sided shed yourself using a few ply woods. It's important to note that you should place the kennel where there are no prevailing winds and draughts. Pigs can only tolerate a temperature between 12 – 26 degrees Celsius; otherwise it could be too hot or too cold for their body. This is why blankets are also needed during cold temperatures and a mud hole that they could splash in during hotter days, as they don't sweat, so they need to cool off. With that being said, your crate or kennel should at least have 8 square feet of space with rough unfinished flooring – it's good for their hooves. It is also recommended for you to have a cemented space for them to get some exercise or sun bathe if they need to, plus it could prevent smelly conditions as well.

Do not completely cement everything or let them sleep on a concrete floor all the time, as it is not good for their bones; their bodies thrive on the ground. Another important note you need to remember is to make sure that you provide enough shade or roofing for your pig so that they won't get sunburned or dehydrated.

'Play Space' or Pen Space

A pig's natural instinct is to play or root in the mud and holes because that's where they get their nutrients and vitamins. Do not discourage them from doing so. However, for the purpose of cleanliness around your house, you should also regulate the amount of mud they would jump in, as you don't want dirt around your house all the time. You can provide your pigs a playpen to stay in without compromising their natural habitat needs.

If you don't want to let your pigs run loose in the house, you should provide a pen space in addition to your kennel. As mentioned earlier, pigs love to move freely and roam around; you should not restrict that because that is a form of exercise for them. A pigpen should be secured using a fence, preferably buy a breezeblock wall around the shed that will serve as a pig-proof gate. You can also use wire-fence but it is expensive and usually ineffective. Make sure that your fence is tight; pigs can spot a weakness and could use that opening to get out of his shed or kennel.

2) Recommended Kennel Accessories

In addition to providing your pig with a kennel and pen space, you also need to stock it with certain accessories. Here are a few things your pig needs for its habitat:

Water Bowl

When it comes to your pig's water bowl, the larger the better, and a flat surface is preferred to prevent it from tipping. Provide as much water as possible because pigs need to be hydrated at all times, as they don't have sweat glands so aside from stumping themselves into the mud, they need lots of water to cool off.

Food Bowl

Food dishes for pigs come in all shapes and sizes but you should choose a set that suits your pet's needs. Pot-bellied pigs are relatively small breeds, so don't choose anything too large. As mentioned in the previous chapters, stainless steel and ceramic bowls do not harbor bacteria like plastic can and they are easy to clean. Try and get the non-tipping versions of the bowl. Pigs love to tip things over and forage around, so if they learn from a very young age that they are unable to tip the bowl over, then they will remember that throughout their life.

Hayrack

It is recommended that you buy a hayrack where you can place hay for your pig. Pigs love to nest and root in hay because it's a natural instinct.

Litter Pan

Your pig's litter pan does not need to be anything fancy – it just needs to be large enough for your pig to turn around in and deep enough to contain the litter without making it hard for your pig to get into the pan. Make sure that you train your pig to identify which is the litter pan and the water bowl; you need to constantly replace the contents of the bowls.

Bedding

Your pig also needs a hiding place or shelter and of course a bedding. You may need to consider the type of litter you want to use for your pig's bedding, if you choose to use any at all. The best litter to use as mentioned earlier is fresh hay, ideally edible hay like meadow hay or timothy hay. You can also use a straw or blanket made from some kind of natural fiber. If you're living in an apartment and your kennel is in a concrete floor, then make sure to place a rubber mat so that you can hose off the dirt. It's very important to put a lot of bedding sheets for your pig because as mentioned earlier, sleeping on concrete floors is not suitable for them.

3) Should I Get A Hutch Or A Cage?

Whether you buy a hutch or a cage, your pot-bellied pig should have somewhere to live that is dry and warm. If you live in a city block apartment you will need a cage, but if you live somewhere with a backyard you could have a hutch. The positioning of their 'house' should be in a draught-free spot, that doesn't get that noisy. The size of the hutch or cage will depend on how many pot-bellied pigs you're getting and what size they are likely to grow to. Remember pot belly pigs have fairly poor eyesight and can't see clearly past a meter. For this reason, you don't want to have a hutch that is too big, as they may feel uncomfortable with not being able to see the corners, as they may think something else is there.

Top Tips For Choosing A Hutch:
- Make sure the hutch is sturdy and well made.
- Check that any paint or varnish is pet-friendly.
- Make sure it's the right size, and not too small; remember your pet will grow.
- Ideally the floor should be wooden. Many people think wire floors are a bad idea as the pot-bellied pig could get its foot caught in it.
- A hutch with legs is best, as it raises the hutch off the floor a little distance and this reduces the risk of dampness inside the hutch.

Top Tips For Choosing A Cage:
- The cage should ideally have a space where the pot-bellied pig can hide if it wants to.
- It should be spacious.
- It should be easy to clean.

- If any paint or varnish has been used it should be pet friendly.
- There shouldn't really be 'grid-like' flooring - this is for the same reason as stated above in the hutch part.

4) Pot-bellied Pig Bedding

Bedding for Hutches
As a hutch is likely to be in a cooler environment than a cage, more bedding will be needed to keep your pet warm.

- Sawdust or soft wood shavings. This can be used as a base layer, about one to two inches thick. This will act as an absorbent for urine. Some people have found that their pot-bellied pigs are allergic to this material – if this is the case don't use it. Such allergies to wood shavings are often caused by urine reacting with chemicals that have been added to shavings producing phenols, which can result in skin complaints and other problems, such as respiratory complications. Seek a vet's opinion if you notice anything worrying. I use sawdust as a base layer (with hay on top) for all my pot-bellied pigs and have not as yet found any problem, but you should always check if your pot-bellied pigs are allergic before using a lot of it.

- Hay. You should cover the base of the hutch (or apply on top of the sawdust/wood shavings) with a generous supply of hay. You should have a lot more in the sleeping compartment than in the main compartment, as pot-bellied pigs (especially baby pot-bellied pigs) like to burrow a lot. A lot of pot-bellied pigs will eat some of their hay, as it is a good source of fiber, so extra should always be put out every day if the pot-bellied pig hasn't enough to eat and use as bedding. Thicker, courser hay can be added to the sleeping compartment in the winter to provide more substantial bedding and help the pot-bellied pigs keep warm.

Warning: Never use straw. It is quite sharp and rough and can stick in the pot-bellied pig's skin. Cavies have very sensitive skin and straw has been known to cause skin complaints.

Make sure you remove any soiled bedding regularly and clean out the cage, replacing it with fresh, clean bedding. As mentioned before, pigs are very clean animals and as such prefer to live in a clean environment – especially one which is where they sleep and is their personal refuge.

Tips: Before you put any bedding down, line the hutch with newspaper – this will make it easier to clean out next time. Alternatively, stick a pet-friendly lino down with non-toxic glue to the floor of the hutch – this will help preserve the wood and make it easier to sweep out soiled bedding. Newspaper can be used on top of this lino.

Bedding for Cages

Here you have two options:
- The first would be to use the bedding that you'd use in a hutch: sawdust, hay and newspaper/lino (see above for more details). This is probably the best type of bedding to use, as hay is a natural material and the pot-bellied pig can also eat some of it if he or she is hungry.

- The second type of bedding sometimes used in cages is shredded paper, or newspaper. This isn't the best type of bedding to use, as it isn't that substantial and won't be that good at keeping your pet warm (although a cage should be inside the house anyway). Another problem with using shredded paper is that the pot-bellied pig could get ink poisoning if they eat it, which could be fairly likely in some pot-bellied pigs.

Whichever type of bedding you choose to use for your pot-bellied pig's cage, you should have an area, ideally cornered off or inside a separate box, where there is a lot more bedding for the pot bellypig to burrow down in at night. Baby pot-bellied pigs especially love to burrow. The cornered off area will also provide an area where your pet can get some privacy.

Tip: Some owners choose to line the cage with newspaper or stick a animal-friendly-lino down (with non toxic glue), as this makes it easier to clean out the next time. Obviously the newspaper would have to be replaced every time.

Warning: Some pot-bellied pigs are allergic to sawdust. If this is the case, don't use it. Don't use any materials that have had harmful or non-pet-friendly chemicals added to them.

5) Cleaning Out Hutches And Cages

Your pot-bellied pig will need it's hutch or cage cleaned at least once a week, but what is the best way to do it? Here is a quick guide on the best way to clean out a hutch or cage:

1) Remove the pot-bellied pigs and put them in a safe place.
2) Remove any bowls and toys.
3) Fold the newspaper inwards, so the bedding is inside, then lift it out and put in a carrier bag ready for disposal.
4) Next, using a brush specifically for this purpose, sweep out any remaining bedding and dispose of it.
5) Spray the hutch or cage with pet friendly disinfectant and leave to dry.
6) Once the hutch is dry, spread down new newspaper.
7) Add a layer of sawdust.
8) Next add some hay. Don't use straw, as this can be quite sharp on a pot-bellied pig's sensitive skin. This especially applies to baby pot belly pigs, as they tend to burrow more.
9) Clean out the food bowls, making sure they are washed, rinsed and dried to remove any old food particles that might be remaining. Sometimes a pig will urinate or defecate in its water source – so make sure that the water bowl/sources of water are checked at least on a daily basis and replaced with fresh water.
10) Place back the food bowls and refill them after tipping any old food out. Put back the toys.

Chapter 6. Basic Training

1) Potty Training for Pot-bellied Pigs

Pot-bellied pigs, especially young piglets, do not have full bladder control, so if you don't want any litter around your house, you have to train them while they're young. When it comes to potty training you have three options; you can use a litter pan inside, train them to poop outside, or both. Usually it's better to do both. Changes in the weather may not permit your pig to defecate outside, so that's why you should train them to use a litter pan inside the house.

Young pigs need to start off with small litter boxes or pans until they are old enough to litter outside. Pigs do not want to soil their shed, so it's better to put the litter box in a corner far away from where they sleep or eat but near enough so that they can easily find and remember it.

Installing a doggy door is also a good idea – with the intention that the pig then has the choice of going outside, or using its litter tray inside the house. Remember, when training your pig to use either the litter tray, or accompanying it outside – always allow time for it to finish – and that it should both urinate and empty its bowels. Whilst it is in the act, use a phrase such as "go potty", or whichever phrase you prefer. Once finished, remember to praise your pig with a kind phrase, affection and a treat. Make sure you give the treat in a timely manner – not too soon, or too late – so that it associates a successful potty trip with a reward.

If using a doggy door in order to train your pet pig to go outside to potty, always ensure the route to the doggy door is clear and free of obstacles, so the pig can easily access it and reduce the risk of accidents inside the home.

Here are some tips on how to potty train your pig inside the house:

▪ Put them in their potty box as often as possible, ideally after they eat and drink. Use reinforcement training and say "go potty," they're intelligent creatures so if you make potty training in a litter a habit they will surely retain it.

- Make sure the litter pan is low enough so that your pig can easily enter.
- Do not change the potty spot as much as possible; make it a permanent litter spot for your pig. Once they have learned where the spot is, they will always go there to poop because they have already developed it as a habit.
- Be prepared for "potty accidents" on the carpet or flooring.
- Make sure your pot-bellied pig has mastered their potty training before you let them roam around your house.

Here are some tips on how to potty train your pig outside the house:

- Put up a confined or small area where they can poop. After eating or drinking, take them outside to their designated potty area. Use positive reinforcement, say phrases such as "good girl/boy" as well as commands such as "go poop"
- It's better to give them treats after they have successfully pooped outside. It will also help if you consistently take them outside when pooping for the first few weeks until they have mastered going on their potty spot by themselves.

2) Socializing and Training Your Pot-bellied Pig

At some point in time, you and your pet will already get along and be comfortable with each other. Strengthen your relationship by taming them through training. Training a pot-bellied pig is not that hard to do, in fact it can be a fun and rewarding bonding experience for both of you.

There are lots of pet owners out there who have properly trained and raised a well-behaved pot-bellied pig. They are intelligent creatures that are highly motivated by food and routines. Trust is the most important key in training your pot-bellied pig. The first thing you need to do is to be able to establish a solid connection and rapport between you and your pet. This section will provide some guidelines you can follow to get your pot-bellied pig well behaved and disciplined. Remember, as with any domestic pet you are wishing to train, the key is patience, reward and discipline.

If you are a new pig owner, it may take some practice to teach them some basic skills. One thing you can do is use small and healthy treats such as non-buttered and non-salted popcorn, wheat, cheerios, or small chunks of fruits to entice your pot-bellied pig to come to you and follow your command. Aside from using treats, you should also set specific time during the day for your training because pigs also liked routines. It is advisable to train them before bedtime so that they will have a good night's sleep. Physical and mental workouts are best done when your pig is focused, so don't do it right after eating their meal or when they are hungry. Make sure you are in patient frame of mind, and pick a time where you can both concentrate – and most importantly, enjoy! – the task at hand.

Before starting the training that day, give both yourself and the pig a few minutes – the pig will then be able to turn its attention away from what it was doing, before commencing the session of training. Be flexible! Be prepared for things not to go entirely to plan with the training at times, or even not at all – but always ensure that you end a training session on a positive note! Remember that timely reward. If the training session that day really isn't going well, there is no point getting upset and frustrated. Just stop for a while or even start it over another day. Do be aware of the pig's physical limitations – they do not have the agility of dogs due to their own body shape, so you will have to spend more time and effort on certain things until they become accustomed to whatever you are trying to teach them.

Handle your pig gently and with care, using a scooping motion to pick it up. You may find if the pig wasn't handled very much from birth that it may react negatively by "screaming" or struggling. If that's the case, put it down – but continue with picking it up at various times of the day for short durations in order for it to become accustomed to being handled by you. Again, when the pig is not struggling or screaming in your arms after each successful, short attempt at holding it, remember to give it a treat and praise it.

Equally, if your pig is displaying behavior which could be damaging, such as digging its hooves into furniture – a light tap on the pig's nose and a firm "no" from you a few times will quickly be learned and understood. Remember that pigs have excellent memories! You should never physically hurt your pig – a gentle tap on its nose with a firm "no" is sufficient – and repeated to discourage unwanted behavior will be enough for it to learn – reaching a point when the word "no" will be enough for it to behave itself. Other techniques for discouraging inappropriate behavior is to use a can filled with marbles or small stones or water pistol/water sprayer. If you are some distance away from your pig when bad behavior occurs, you can throw the can in the pig's direction (not at the pig!) and saying a firm "no".

This method can be used outside or inside. If you are outside and the pig is displaying bad behavior, fill a water pistol/water sprayer with water and spray it into the pig's mouth (not into its eyes!) to distract it – again followed quickly by a firm "no". You will need to repeat either of these techniques a few times until they are able to be corrected just by using the word "no". You will need to be consistent. Remember, correct bad behaviour and reward good behaviour! Both, however, in a timely manner.

Chapter 7. Grooming Your Pot-bellied Pigs

Different pot-bellied pig breeds may have different coat conditions and textures, so take the time to explore your pig's coat in order to determine what his grooming needs might be. Grooming your pot-bellied pig helps to distribute the natural body oils to keep his skin healthy, shiny, and soft. No matter what kind of coat your pot-bellied pig has, it is your job to groom it properly so it remains in good health. In this chapter you will learn the basics about grooming your pot-bellied pig; this includes brushing and bathing your pig as well as trimming his hooves or nails, cleaning his tusk, and brushing his teeth.

1) Is It Really Necessary to Bathe your Pot-bellied Pig?

Yes, this is one of the most debated issues related to pot-bellied pig care. Many experts say that there is no need to regularly bathe your pot-bellied pig as they clean themselves. Yet, many people do wash their pot-bellied pigs from time to time to keep them in good condition. By nature, pigs love to be around water and provided that they are very young when introduced, this can be a fun experience for the both of you.

Sometimes, you might find that some pot-bellied pigs simply cannot stand being washed. If this is the case then it is probably advisable not to wash them. Of course there are pot-bellied pigs who love bath time, if this is the case with one of your pot-bellied pigs then it is OK to give them baths about once a month. Remember to limit the time it takes to give a bath to your pot-bellied pig, as you don't want a piggy to get too cold or wet, as this could make them ill. You can put toys in the water for them to "nose", a few vegetable leaves for them to root around with and don't forget to praise and administer treats – make it a pleasurable experience for them!

When they are used to being in the water, it is at that time you can gently massage their skin with a small brush or sponge. Clean the pig's feet and hooves and tummy area to remove any dirt, urine or fecal matter – and don't be surprised if the pig defecates in the water as this is perfectly normal behavior! A child's paddling pool outside in good weather is a great alternative to using the bath inside the house. Just a couple of inches of water will suffice. Never over-bathe your pig as that can cause the skin to become dry, flaky and itchy.

Make sure to apply a moisturizing skin oil as a spray whilst the skin is still damp or apply a small amount of lotion when the skin is dry. The lotion or oil needs to absorb into the skin – otherwise it will transfer to everything else the pig comes into contact with after bath time!

If you get a longhaired pot-bellied pig then it will need daily brushing to prevent tangles in the fur. It is important that this is done because otherwise feces could get stuck in the tangles - if this happens and you are unable to get it out without hurting the pot-bellied pig then it will probably need to have that part of fur shaved off by the vet, so it is best to avoid tangles in the fur.
Shorthaired pot belly pigs will obviously need little brushing, although you will still need to check for any tangles that may have formed. Pet brushes can be bought from most pet shops for this purpose.

REMEMBER: brush in the direction of the fur as it is naturally. This can be quite challenging if your pot-bellied pig has rosettes, (fur that sticks up at all angles).

2) Recommended Tools for Grooming
In order to keep your pig's coat clean and in good condition you will need to have a few grooming tools on hand. Since pigs have a short coat and are hypoallergenic (they don't have fur, just hairs) you don't need to buy a brush.

Here are some of the grooming tools that may come in handy when it comes to grooming and bathing your pot-bellied pig:
Soap
Shampoo
Lotion
Hard wire cutter
Large nail cutter
Metal File
Rasp

Toothbrush
Baking Soda/Toothpaste
Baby Wipes
Sponge or soft small brush with handle
Waterproof bath toys (safe ones that young children use in the bath)

Learning how to groom your pot-bellied pig effectively is a task that takes time to learn. If you have no idea where to start or how to do it, it wouldn't be a bad idea to talk to a fellow pot-bellied pig owner or take your pot-bellied pig to a professional groomer so that they can show you what to do. You can also consult your vet for some tips. In the next section, you will be provided with an overview on how to easily clean your pig.

3) Tips for Bathing and Grooming Pot-bellied Pigs
Unlike other pets or animals, pot-bellied pigs and pigs in general love to splash in the water and take a bath. They will surely enjoy it and for sure you will too.

Some owners bathe their pot-bellied pigs once or twice a day. Ideally, you want to do it in the morning after they eat breakfast or midday (after playtime) and after dinner so that they won't be covered in food or dirt before bedtime. You can also clean their noses using baby wipes. Pigs don't need to have a long bath; it could only take about 10 – 15 minutes and the water should be lukewarm. There are no restrictions when it comes to the kind of soap, shampoo and even lotion you can use. Whatever works for humans is also often applicable for your pig pet. However, before applying any soap or shampoo, make sure to check the chemical content first. It is also wise to ask your vet the kinds of bathing products are good to use on your pig.

When bathing be extra careful to not let the soap or shampoo get into their eyes. You can also use a germ oil to keep mites away from your pig and keep its coat healthy and soft.
Bathe your pig regularly; you can also bathe them in your bathtub (make sure to provide a rubber mat so that your pot-bellied pig won't slip). Keep in mind that a cooling bath or playtime in the bathtub helps in bringing down your pig's body temperature because

they can't sweat on their own. After bathing you can use a soft towel or cloth to dry them off.

Grooming sessions are a great way for you to bond with your pig, so make it fun for you and your pet.

4) Trimming Your Pot Belly Pig's Hoofs

Like human nails, pot belly pig's nails or claws are constantly growing and therefore need to be clipped or trimmed on a regular basis. The ease of this will depend on the pot-bellied pig in question. From experience, I have found that you'll get a couple who will play up, a couple who don't mind, and others that will be fine one time and not-so-fine the next time. Some don't like the feeling and may try to bite, so be prepared.

A good rule of thumb, especially if you own a pot-bellied pig from a baby is that as with any domestic pet, get them used to having their feet (hooves) and ears handled from a young age and on a regular basis. They will become accustomed to being touched in those areas and that will make it so much easier for you during the grooming process and any vet visits when they require treatment. With the hooves, handle them gently at first, then try applying a light pressure to the nail area. This will mimic the feeling of the pressure applied by clipping the nails. The pig will become comfortable with this process over time, making the job so much easier for you.

Pot-bellied pigs have a total of 14 nails, 4 on each front paw, and 3 on each back paw. I have found that the nails on the back legs tend to grow quicker and straighter, whereas the nails on the front paws are more likely to curl up.

Some pot-bellied pigs will need their nails trimmed less often than others, particularly if they are getting a lot of exercise. You should always keep an eye on how long your pot-bellied pig's nails are. Broken nails can be very painful for a pot-bellied pig and can result in an infection.

I would say that a pot-bellied pig's nails should first be trimmed when they are 2-4 months old. The smaller the pot-bellied pig, the harder it is likely to be to trim the nails. Older pot belly pigs tend to have nails that are tougher and grow at irregular speeds.

When trimming the nails, make sure you have a firm hold on your pot-bellied pig, as some may try to get away.

To trim a pot-bellied pig's claws you need to make sure you have suitable nail clippers. Pot-bellied pig nail clippers can be bought from most pet shops, animal stores, garden centers that have a pet section, and sometimes vets.

There are several different types of nail clippers; as a pot-bellied pig owner you should find one that suits you and your pot-bellied pig(s) the best. Some owners use nail clippers designed for humans, although I find these harder to use on such small nails. I use scissor nail clippers that have been designed for kittens and other small animals. It is possible to use dog nail trimmers as well, although there is a danger you'll cut off too much if the clippers are large. Whichever type of nail clipper you use, you should always be very careful when cutting your pot-bellied pig's nails. You don't want to cut too deep and into the 'quick' – this is the end of the blood vessel and if cut it will bleed a lot, and in some cases can be very painful and cause an infection. With light colored nails you can see where the blood vessel ends, as it looks pink, so it is easier to cut these nails. Darker nails are harder, so it is more advisable to cut small sections off, rather than doing it all in one go, until you've cut the desired amount of. With some dark nails, if you shine a bright light from underneath it will sometimes show where the quick ends.

If your pot belly pig has very long nails it is likely that the quick is also very long. In this case, you should still only cut off the tip of the nail to stop the quick from bleeding. This long nail should be regularly trimmed, about once or twice a week, having a little taken off each time, as this encourages the blood vessel to recede.

Every now and then you may find that you have cut slightly too deep; this may be because you couldn't see the quick or the pot-bellied pig moved. In this case you should wait until the nail has stopped bleeding before putting the pig back in his or her hutch. To reduce the chance of infection you should clean the pot-bellied pig's hutch or cage out so there will be less contact with soiled bedding. If the nail has not stopped bleeding for over 5 minutes, or is badly cut, I would suggest taking the pot-bellied pig to a vet just to be on the safe side.

It is advisable to get advice about cutting pot-bellied pig nails from an experienced owner or a vet if this is the first time you have done it. If you don't feel confident enough to cut your piggy's nails then it would be best to get a trained vet to do it. The information I have provided cannot be taken as a medical opinion or medical advice. Remember, only an adult should ever cut a pot-bellied pig's nails.

5) Trimming Your Pot-bellied Pig's Tusk

Male (or boar) pot-bellied pigs, like normal sized pigs, have tusks. They can either be trimmed or not. You can trim your pig's tusk depending on what kind of breed it is, how long it grows over time and the risk for people as well. Tusks may grow rapidly depending on the breed and often these are sharp; that's why it could dangerous to people, especially for owners with small children. A boar will often rub and hone its tusks until they get very sharp – and inadvertently cause serious injury to other animals and people.

The schedule of tusk trimming is entirely up to you. Some owners do it once a year, others on a monthly basis, while others still only do it when necessary. It's better to bring your pot-bellied pig to the vet if you want its tusks to be trimmed; you need an expert for this because if you try to do it yourself and hurt the pig they could suffer from trauma and experience Porcine Stress Syndrome, which is fatal. Once you bring your pet to the vet, you can also discuss anesthesia options to aid in the tusk trimming.

6) Caring for Your Pot Belly Pig's Teeth

You can leave the brushing of your pot-bellied pig's teeth to a professional groomer or vet, but in case you want to cut the expenses, you can do it yourself. You just need to provide a toothbrush (ideally a pet toothbrush but human toothbrushes are fine) and toothpaste that doesn't contain fluoride – fluoride can be poisonous to your pet; baking soda is preferred.

Just like in trimming your pot-bellied pig's tusk and hooves, it's better to start brushing their teeth while they are still young so that it will be easier for you when they're older because they'll be used to it. Piglets start to grow teeth when they are about one year old. You can carefully touch their teeth and put your fingers slowly inside their mouth until they are comfortable with it, then you can start brushing them. Be careful though; you don't want to hurt their gums. You can also use a washcloth for brushing. But watch your fingers as they might try and nip you in the early stages. Again, it's best to get your pet pig used to being handled in all areas as soon as possible. Be sure to keep a close eye on any broken teeth or signs of infection in the gums. Again, if a problem has been left too long and a veterinarian is required, it may be necessary to sedate or use an anesthetic in order to treat the problem.

7) Cleaning your Pot-bellied Pig's Ears

You will need to regularly check your pig's ears for signs of infection or parasites. Normally that will show itself by a nasty odour which you can pick up by gently cleaning inside the ear with a cotton swab. Be extremely careful whilst doing this, as any sudden movement from the pig could cause injury. If you do find signs of infection, or parasites, speak to your vet who can supply specific antibiotic or insecticidal lotions for them. Make sure also that after bathing, there is no water left in the ears and that they are dry, as this can be a breeding ground for bacteria and cause infection. Cotton swabs dipped in a rubbing alcohol and gently wiping around the inside of the ear is enough to clean and check for problems. Also, you will find that your pig enjoys the sensation – as it's akin to scratching and rubbing themselves which is a pleasurable thing to do. Remember, again – to praise and give your pig a treat!

Chapter 8. Keeping Your Pot-bellied Pig Healthy

You as the owner should be aware of the potential threats and diseases that could harm the wellness of your pot-bellied pig. Just like human beings, you need to have knowledge on these diseases so that you can prevent it from happening in the first place. In this section you will find tons of information on the most common problems that may affect your pig including its causes, signs and symptoms, remedies and prevention. While you may not be able to prevent your pig from getting sick in certain situations, you can be responsible in educating yourself about the diseases that could affect your pot-bellied pig.

The more you know about these potential health problems, the better you will be able to identify them and to seek immediate veterinary care when needed.

Make sure you get to know your pig's metabolic rates. The normal temperature for a pig is between 102-103.6 degrees F (28.8-39.8 degrees C). Some pigs have normal variations of these temperatures – so in order to become familiar with it, make sure that you take its temperature at the same time for a few days, when it is neither excited or active, in order to get its normal range. Then you will know that whenever the temperature increases slightly above that (and it's not excited or active in order to cause that raise in temperature), then it is most likely to be sick. At this point you can then take the appropriate action.

1) Common Health Problems Affecting Pot-bellied Pigs

Pet pot belly pigs can be affected by a number of different health problems and they are generally not specific to any particular breed. Feeding your pig a nutritious diet will go a long way in ensuring his total health and wellbeing, but sometimes pot belly pigs get sick anyway. If you want to make sure that your pig gets the treatment he needs as quickly as possible you need to learn how to identify the symptoms of disease. These symptoms are not always obvious either; your pot-bellied pig may not show any outward signs of illness except for a subtle change in behavior.

The more time you spend with your pet pig, the more you will come to understand his behavior – this is the key to catching health problems early. At the first sign that something is wrong with your pot-bellied pig you should take a note of his symptoms, both physical and behavioral, so you can relay them to your veterinarian who will then make a diagnosis and prescribe a course of treatment. The sooner you identify these symptoms, the sooner your vet can take action and the more likely your pot-bellied pig will be able to make a full recovery.

Pot-bellied pigs are prone to a wide variety of different diseases, though some are more common than others. For the benefit your pot-bellied pig's long-term health, take the time to learn the causes, symptoms, and treatment options for some of the most common health problems.

Below are some of the most common health problems that can occur in pot-bellied pigs. You will learn some guidelines on how these diseases can be prevented and treated as well as its signs and symptoms. Remember, as you spend more and more time with your pet pig, you will become very accustomed to its personality and behavior – so you will be the first person to notice when things aren't quite right with it. Sometimes, a pet pig will show no real signs of illness at first, that is why it is absolutely essential to understand and become very familiar with it in order to detect the first signs of any illness, which you can then take action on.

1. Dippity Pig Syndrome
Dippity Pig Syndrome is also referred to as Erythema Multiforme or Bleeding Back Syndrome. This syndrome is an acute skin condition that is usually found along the backs of pot-bellied pigs and it is very common among piglets (around 4 months old). It can be very painful for your pet if not treated immediately.

Causes
Up until now, researchers and veterinarians cannot determine the cause of Dippity Pig Syndrome, however, some scientists say that

this could somehow come from the herpes virus and there is some evidence from biopsy tests that it is genetic and occurs in the pigs' lineage.

Signs and Symptoms
There are a lot of signs that your pot-bellied pig or piglets have Dippity Pig Syndrome. If you notice your pet always screaming in pain, having a temporary dipping of its hind legs, or have sores on its back, it's a sure indicator that your pet is suffering from this illness. Other symptoms include showing red stripes along its back and a sudden change in its attitude.

Prevention and Treatment
There is no actual treatment for this syndrome, but the good thing is that the pain is only temporary and it only lasts for about 4 days max. Usually the onset of symptoms occurs suddenly and without warning and disappears as suddenly – sometimes within 24-48 hours. It can appear very frightening. However, you can take simple measures to help your pet become comfortable during this painful process. You can reduce the stress around him by providing comfortable bedding, soft music and also try to isolate them from other pets or even people so that they can rest. You can also give some medication such as a buffered aspirin or a Tylenol. Your vet could also give you something like Tramadol to reduce the pain; it's better to bring your pet to the vet so that they can give the proper medication your pot-bellied pig needs.

2. Urinary Tract Infection
UTI is very common in pets and pot-bellied pigs are no exception. Of course, different pig breeds will show different symptoms and would also be given different treatment. If you think something is not right with your pot belly pig, it's safe to assume that he/she might have a UTI, just take a urine sample and bring it to the vet.

Causes
UTI can be caused by stress, heat cycle or hormonal changes, various infections, and bladder or kidney stones.

Signs and Symptoms

Clinical signs of UTI in pot-bellied pigs include frequent urination, fever, change in the color and odor of the urine, irritability, loss of appetite, and lethargy.

Prevention and Treatment

If your pot belly pig has a UTI or if you think the symptoms are caused by UTI, you need to take your pig to your vet as soon as possible. It would be better if you could obtain a fresh urine sample of your pet and have your vet analyze it for infection or abnormalities. The usual treatment for UTI is antibiotics. Always make sure there is fresh water on hand for your pig, to keep it hydrated.

3. Pig Fever

Just like in humans, fever is an indicator that something is wrong in the body.

Causes

If your pet pig has a fever, chances are he/she has a viral or bacterial infection, allergies, or inflammation, has ingested a toxin or was bitten by bugs or insects.

Signs and Symptoms

The most common sign of fever is of course the rise of its body temperature. Just like in humans, it's the body's self-defense to wipe out the bacterial or viral infection, so if your pot-bellied pig's body temperature doesn't drop no matter what first aid medicines you give to him or her, that only means that it's not caused by an infection. Bring your pet immediately to the veterinarian.

Treatment

If your pig has a fever and you can't immediately bring it to your vet you can administer first aid treatment. You can increase its fluid intake; try offering fruit juices such as apple or cranberries and also a few meals. You can also give them ice cubes wrapped up in ice packs if in case he/she wants to cool itself down. It's important that you don't give them a full bath at this time. Do not give them any kind of aspirin, but you may try offering them a Tylenol every 8 hours for at least 3 days. If symptoms persist more than 3 days, consult your vet.

4. Abscesses

An abscess is a pocket of fluid and pus generally caused by a bacterial infection. These are fairly common in pot-bellied pigs as well as farm pigs in general because they can form anywhere on the pig's body.

Causes

The cause of an abscess could be any number of things including a bite, a cut, or some other kind of wound – they may also be caused by foreign bodies becoming embedded in the pigs' skin.

Signs and Symptoms

Abscesses can be very painful for your pot-bellied pig and it may cause him to stop eating or lose his appetite. He may also drool and drop bits of food when he does eat. Abscesses on the skin usually appear as hard lumps. You may find that he rubs a particular area or starts chewing that area of infection.

Prevention and Treatment

The best treatment for an abscess is to drain the fluid and pus, which is usually performed under general anesthesia. Following the drainage, the wound must be kept clean and painkillers may also be prescribed; it's better to discuss options with your veterinarian.

5. Ringworm

Ringworm or intestinal worms is another common illness for pigs. You may not completely be aware of it, so it's better for your pot-bellied pig, especially piglets, to undergo a deworming process to prevent further illnesses.

Signs and Symptoms

If your pot-bellied pig has intestinal worms, there won't be any visible signs, but you can always check their poop every now and then. If you see worms that look like pasta or threads, that's a sign that your pot-bellied pig has a lot of ringworms. You won't notice physical symptoms until they have affected your pig's immune system.

Prevention and Treatment

To prevent the spread of ringworm or other intestinal parasites, you may want to deworm your pig as early as 6 weeks old. You can also do it twice a year or every 6 months for prevention. You can buy over the counter treatments such as Doramectin or Fenbendazole to deworm your pig. Consult your vet for further specifications.

6. Pneumonia

Pneumonia is another common illness in pigs, especially in young pot-bellied pigs. It is generally caused by some kind of infection, bacterial or viral in most cases, which leads to inflammation in the lungs.

Causes

Pneumonia can result from four different types of infections. It can either be bacterial, viral, fungal, or parasitic. It is also possible for environmental factors such as chemicals, smoke, or dental disease to cause inflammation, which leads to pneumonia. Usually climate conditions also affect piglets.

Signs and Symptoms

Pneumonia in animals has symptoms such as sneezing, nasal discharge, fever, anorexia, weight loss, eye discharge, drooling, and difficulty breathing.

Prevention and Treatment

The type of infection will determine the severity of the disease as well as the proper course of treatment. Piglets suffering from pneumonia may not survive. Your vet may also prescribe antiviral, antimicrobial, antifungal, or antibiotic medications depending on the type of infection causing your pig's pneumonia.

7. Scabies

Scabies or otherwise known as Sarcoptic Mange is caused by an external parasites known as mites. These are microscopic parasites that invade and infect the skin's pig. It is one of the most common problems with pot-bellied pigs and farm pigs as well.

Causes

The cause of a scabies infestation is still unknown, but it is likely that some pigs carry the mites unknowingly and problems only develop when pigs are weakened by stress, illness, or injury. Mites feed on keratin, which leads to poor coat condition and skin quality. Obviously frequent physical contact with your pet pig and with bathing regularly, you will notice changes in its skin condition.

Signs and Symptoms

The most common signs of scabies in pigs are head and ear shaking, the development of tiny, pimple-like allergies, and excessive scratching that leads to severe rubbing of the skin that causes bleeding. It may take approximately three weeks before symptoms appear but sometimes it could take months before these signs are noticed.

Prevention and Treatment

Treatment for scabies generally involves medication via Dectomax or Ivermectin injection or mixing it with the pigs food. Consult your vet if symptoms persist. Regular grooming or bathing will also help prevent reinfection.

2) Preventing Illness

In addition to learning about the different diseases to which your pot-bellied pig may be prone, there are some other simple things you can do to keep your pet healthy. For one thing, you need to keep your pig's pen clean. Not only will cleaning your pig's playpen help to prevent the spread of parasites, bacteria, and other harmful pathogens, but it will also help to keep your pig's stress level low. If your pig becomes stressed, it could compromise his immune system and he may be more likely to get sick if he is exposed to some kind of illness. It is important to note that you should also be mindful of making sure that your pig gets the right vaccinations and you should take steps to protect your pot belly pig against parasites.

In this section you will find guidelines on how you can prevent unwanted illnesses that could endanger your pig's life. Always give your pig a healthy, nutritious diet – pay particular care to the proteins, vitamins and minerals that your pet needs. A healthy diet makes a healthy pet.

Try not to let your pet pig socialize with other pigs or animals that are not yours. Cross contamination of illnesses could occur – and be especially aware that other people's animals or pet pigs may not follow the same vaccination procedures as yours, or perhaps they haven't been as diligent as you in the health care of their pet(s). Never let them eat or drink from other animals' water or food bowls. If you ever travel with your pet, make sure you take your own – and if possible, also take along its own cage and bedding. When you return home, make sure to thoroughly clean and disinfect their equipment. Also, clean your pet once home as soon as possible – they could be carrying fecal matter, bacteria, parasites and their eggs on their feet which can easily be transferred to their home environment.

Sanitize Your Pot-bellied Pig's Cage
When it comes to cleaning your pot-bellied pig's cage, you want to disinfect everything. Start by emptying everything out of your pig's playpen or kennel – that includes bedding, food bowls, and blanket and, of course, your pot-bellied pig. After cleaning out your pig's kennel, disinfect it with a pig-friendly cleaner or just simply buy a safe spray, which you can get at the grocery store. After cleaning and disinfecting your pig's kennel you need to do the same for his food and water equipment as well as other accessories. You may want to wash or scrub the bedding or accessories thoroughly using bleach or other cleaning products suitable for pigs or pets in general.

When you are done cleaning and disinfecting, add some fresh bedding to the pen and put everything back. As long as you keep to a regular schedule, you shouldn't have to clean your pigpen more than once a week. If you think it's necessary, over cleanliness wouldn't hurt.

Exercise your pot-bellied pigs
Exercise is very important for your pot-bellied pigs; remember that in the wild they would be running around foraging for food nearly all the time. Ideally your pot-bellied pig should have a chance to run around at least once a week at the minimum. It is important for them to get enough exercise to keep them healthy. Outdoor pens are ideal for your pot-bellied pig in good weather. Alternatively, if your pet is a house pot-bellied pig, set up a space they can run around in. Ensure there are no wires or dangerous objects anywhere near the pot-bellied pig. Remember pot-bellied pigs can climb, so make sure they cannot climb out of their area.
From personal experience I have found that keeping my pot-bellied pigs in their own shed allows them to run around the floor when I let them out. If you have a similar space undercover why not pick some grass and spread it over the floor.

Some pet shops sell leads and harnesses for pot-bellied pigs - this is a great idea although some pot-bellied pigs may not like being strapped into them at first.

Pot-bellied pigs like to explore. Why not make an obstacle course for your piggy by using a couple of kitchen roll tubes.
Many pot-bellied pigs love to run around with their friends.
If you see your pot-bellied pig doing little twisty jumps this probably means they are 'pop-corning'. Pot-bellied pigs do this when they are very excited and are having fun.

Preventing Parasites
Just like other pets, your pot-bellied pig needs protection against mites and other parasites. If one pig has a parasite or is infected with mites, it will most likely spread to other pigs or even pets near it. Consider protecting your pig with a topical flea control preventive; it is recommended that you ask your veterinarian for recommendations on which brand to use and follow the dosing instructions very carefully.

3) Vaccinations
Pot-bellied pigs need vaccinations, especially while they are still young. These vaccinations will help prevent various illnesses and could also act as a booster for its immune system. Take your pet to the veterinarian to discuss the vaccination program your pet pig needs. Below is a list of common and general vaccines that you should give to your pet:

1) Erysipelas Vaccine
Erysipelas is caused by birds but the disease stays in the soil, therefore posing a threat to your pot-bellied pig. Give your pig an erysipelas vaccine at about 8 weeks old, with a booster in 2 weeks. Then do it on a yearly basis.

2) Tetanus Vaccine
Tetanus is also a threat that is found in the soil, and can also cause infection or even fatality especially when contracted though a scratch or wound on your pot-bellied pig. Give your pig a tetanus vaccine, with a booster in 2 weeks. Then do it every 6 months.

3) Leptospirosis Vaccine

This is carried by the infected urine of animals or pests such as rats and raccoons. It can infect your pot-bellied pig through water contamination. Give your pig a leptospirosis vaccine, with a booster in 2 weeks. Then do it on a yearly basis. Make sure that any water source your pet pig drinks from is clean. Also fence off or avoid contact with areas of standing water that your pet pig could get into.

4) Actinobacillus Pleuropneumoiae Vaccine

This vaccine is given to boost your pig's immune system and it is included as a general vaccine for pot-bellied pigs, especially for breeding pigs, to protect their unborn piglets from various diseases.

5) Rabies Vaccine

Usually rabies vaccines for pot-bellied pigs are the same with as what is used for dogs. It is not mandatory or required for pigs, because they don't really bite people. However, you can still have the option to have them vaccinated. It should be done at 4 months of age, with a booster in 1 year. Then you can do it after every 3 years.

4) General Signs of Possible Illnesses

- Eating Disorders: does your pig show signs of appetite loss or drooling and dropping food?
- Coat: does its coat and skin still feel soft, firm and rejuvenated? If your pig is ill or infected, it show physically on its body and can lead to a poor coat condition or hair loss.
- Mobility: does your pig look like it loses its balance?
- Eyes: are there any discharge in the eyes? Are they swollen?
- Ears: do they swell or droop?
- Respiratory: does your pig have difficulty breathing?
- Nose: does your pig have a watery nasal discharge?
- Overall Physique: does your pig stay active or are there any signs of weakness and deterioration?

5) First Aid Kit In Case of Emergencies

Here are some things that may come in handy when treating minor illnesses in your pot-bellied pig or in case of emergencies. Make sure you have these in your home at all times:

Oatmeal
Canned pumpkin
Karo syrup
Low Sodium Chicken broth
Heat pad
Prilosec or Pepcid
Pepto Bismol
Ivermectin and syringe for worming
Syringes for administering medications
Ice pack
Gatorade or Pedialyte
Digital thermometer
Poison control number
Hydrogen Peroxide 3%
Buffered Aspirin or children's Tylenol
Benedryl
Emergency vet number

Chapter 9. Breeding Your Pot Belly Pigs

Nothing is more adorable than a little baby pot belly pig – except for maybe a whole litter of them! If you decided to buy two pot-bellied pigs, for instance a male and female and keep them together unneutered, you should definitely prepare for the possibility of breeding. If you are interested in breeding your pot-bellied pigs, this chapter will give you a wealth of information about the processes and phases of its breeding and you will also learn how to properly raise pot-bellied pigs on your own.

In addition, if you are interested in becoming a reputable breeder, then this is a must read chapter for you.

1) Top Tips: Breeding Pot-bellied Pigs
Many people love the idea of breeding their pets, but do they know about breeding pot-bellied pigs?
If you want to breed your pot-bellied pigs, there are a few things that you need to know:

If you are thinking about breeding from your pot-bellied pig, then a female (sow) should be bred from for the first time before she is two years old. The reason for this is because, at this age, the hip-bones are just beginning to fuse; if you wait until she is older she is likely to have a lot of trouble delivering the babies, as her hips will have fused together too narrowly, whereas if a female has a litter before she is two years old, her hip-bones would fuse together at this stage, leaving a larger 'space' for delivery.

You should never breed a female who is below 4 months of age. The ideal age to start breeding is 6 to 7 months old or slightly later. Males should be three or four months old, at least, before they are allowed to mate. The heat cycle for a female lasts 16 days. Pregnant sows will need three times the amount of vitamin C that other pot-bellied pigs need.

When a female gives birth, she should ideally be on her own, and definitely away from the male. This is because she is capable of becoming pregnant about four hours after giving birth. Becoming pregnant again, and so soon, is not a good idea for her, as she'll need to nurse her piglets. Stillbirths and miscarriages are quite common in pot-bellied pigs.
The babies can be weaned from the age of 14-28 days. By this time they should weigh between 150 and 200g. The babies will begin to eat a little solid food within the first five days after birth.

2) What To Do With The Babies
Before you breed your pot belly pigs, you should plan what you are going to do with the babies, as they will be your responsibility. You should be prepared to be able to look after all of the pot belly pig babies, as finding a home is not guaranteed. If your pot-bellied pig is expecting a litter, contact pet shops, garden centers, friends, and family to see if anyone would be interested in getting a little pet. Wherever the babies go, it is your responsibility to make sure that they go to a good home where they will be cared for correctly and adequately.

3) Signs that your Pot-bellied Pig is Pregnant:
Usually you won't be able to tell immediately whether your pot-bellied pig or the sow is pregnant unless your veterinarian has done some blood work or if your pot-bellied pig undergoes an ultrasound. This is where most owners gets caught out; sometimes the pigs' belly just naturally appears to be bulky or fatty especially for obese pigs, so you may not notice it until you see some early pregnancy signs.

Within the succeeding weeks, your vet will be able to tell you how many piglets the sow is expecting. It is highly recommended that your pot-bellied pig regularly has a pregnancy check-up so that if ever any problem arises, your vet may be able to assist you because he/she knows your pig's history.

There are behavioral and physical signs that determine if your pot-bellied pig is pregnant. Here are some early signs you need to watch out for:

- The sow may have random mood swings and may become aggressive with other animals for no reason.
- She starts building a nest and will likely want to stay there most of the time.
- The sow also doesn't want to be disturbed and will not want other animals bothering her, even you; be careful because some pigs that are pregnant tend to bite if they are disturbed.
- She may become restless or want chew anything and even try to escape the pen. Make sure she has safe things to chew on in this instance, such as toys and healthy snacks. Also it's vital that you keep on top of changing and replenishing her water source, especially if she is spending more time alone in her "nest".
- Her mammary glands gradually enlarge and become firm. They will also secrete a clear fluid.
- The vulvar lips will start to swell

4) The Labor Process of Pot-bellied Pigs

You will know if your pot-bellied pig is about to give birth if she starts lying on her side. Don't approach her head, but you can at least soothe her and put on calming music because according to research it calms them. The gestation period is around 3 – 4 months. About four days before farrowing or giving birth, the sows' vulva will start to swell. In the next 2 days the breast glands will become tense and will secrete a clear fluid. Within 24 hours, the sow will start to secrete milk, she will be more restless than ever, and her respiration rate will increase. Usually when the sows' mood swings decrease, and if she starts to quietly lay on her side, that's a sign that she will give birth in about an hour.

The sow will then lift her legs up to her belly and her tail will rapidly twitch, after which the straining will begin. You will see a tinge of blood coming out of her vulva; you can expect the first newborn piglet to come out within the next 15 – 20 minutes. Labor duration usually lasts for as short as 30 minutes to as long as 5 hours or more. The placenta is excreted 2 – 4 hours after the last pig was born but a portion of it may come out during farrowing. If the interval time of the piglets delivery exceeds an hour between them, then intervention is necessary.

Important Note
You will need to remain close-by to the new mother and keep a close eye on her to watch her behavior after giving birth. If your pot-bellied pig gave birth for the first time, they may tend to have a temporary weird and aggressive temperament. It may cause them to kill or bite their piglets, which is why you need to remove the piglets away from their mother for a while and slowly put them near her after a few minutes and see how she reacts. Once the sow is tamed, you can lead the other piglets to her for breast-feeding.

5) Caring for Newborn Piglets
Once your pot-bellied pig gives birth, you need to provide more hay than ever. It will serve as a nest for the newborn piglets and a couple of blankets or drying agents will keep them warm. Newborn piglets tend to lose heat very quickly; usually their average temperature is around 100 – 105 degrees Fahrenheit. They should be dried immediately for about 5 minutes after coming out and they should be away from draughts. It is highly recommended that you put a heater or light over the newborns; the temperature should be about 80 to 90 degrees and keep it for at least 8 to 10 days. Piglets cannot produce body heat on their own yet, so it's important to keep them warm.

If you want your piglet to survive and also become healthy in the long run, newborns should be given access to their mother's milk. The colostrum or first milk is needed because it is enriched with immunoglobulin. Allow the pot-bellied pigs to nurse their offspring for about 5 hours or more. Some piglets may be abnormal or disabled; usually these piglets are lighter than average, they are cold or may have splayed legs, some are even anemic; you can identify the anemic pigs by their grayish color. These piglets should be assisted when nursing and when they are drinking milk from their mothers. It is highly recommended that you consult a veterinarian to know the specific procedures for different pot-bellied pig breeds that are disadvantaged.

Chapter 10. Showing Your Pot-bellied Pig

The pot-bellied pig is a wonderful pet to keep but this creature has the potential to be so much more than that. In order to show your pot-bellied pig, however, you have to make sure that he meets the requirements for the breed standard and you need to learn the basics about showing pot-bellied pigs.

In this chapter you will learn more about the specific standard for the pot-bellied pig and receive some tips for entering them in a show. This information will help you to decide if showing your pot-bellied pig is really something you want to do.

1) Preparing Your Pot-bellied Pig for Show

If you will be in an environment that has a lot of pigs and people, make sure that your pot-bellied pig can socialize well.

It's important that you know the rules of show so that you and your pot-bellied pig can act accordingly. It's best that before entering any pot-bellied pig contests you have observed and/or attended previous shows or contests before as part of an audience so that you'll have an idea about how it works. Check the requirements and pig standards so that you know if your pot-bellied pig meets all the requirements for registration.

A few weeks before the show you must have trained your pot-bellied pig to at least have some basic tricks to show off its abilities and discipline (although in costume contests this may not be necessary).

The pot-bellied pig should learn how to listen and follow basic commands. Solidify your pig's grasp of basic obedience and make it learn how to behave so that it won't cause disturbances with other pot-bellied pig participants.

Have your vet clear his overall health before you take it to any show. Take the necessary steps to keep your pig's coat clean and in good condition. You can brush it with soft-bristled brush and spray a mist of water on its hair. Brush off dirt or sand with baby wipes or a soft towel before your pot-bellied pig is called for presentation.

Keep your pot-bellied pig under control; always keep treats in your pocket and walk him or her quietly but with finesse.

Practise standing your pot-bellied pig on a platform – a low table with a small piece of carpet on top so it doesn't slide around is sufficient. Use this technique for short amounts of time every day, to get your pig used to it. Again, remember to praise and give your pig a treat. This technique will also stand you in good stead for when you need to put your pig on an examination table at a veterinary clinic. Your vet will thank you for it! To deal with a calm pig who is used to standing still and being handled for short amounts of time is a huge advantage. It is better for you to pack a bag of supplies that you will need on the day of the show.

This is a list of helpful things to put in your supply pack for your pot belly pig show:
Information for registration
Washing supplies
Brushes or other grooming tools
Small whip (optional)
Rags/towels/baby wipes
Treats and food
Water and food bowls
Trash bags for poop
Medication (if the veterinarian prescribes it)
Clothes for changing
Food and water

If you want to show your pig but you don't want to jump immediately into major competitions, you may be able to find some local pot-bellied pig shows in your area. Local shows may be put on by a branch of a pot-bellied pig breed clubs or associations and they can be a great place to learn and connect with other owners.

To follow on from the disease and illnesses section, please ensure that your pig doesn't come into too close contact with other pigs – and is not allowed to rub against them. Being in a social setting is fine, but do be aware yet again that other pigs may not be on the same vaccination program as yours and may be harboring parasites of viral/bacterial infections. Again, as soon as you get home, it is vital to clean the hooves of your pig to remove anything it may have picked up wandering around, especially if it has walked through fecal matter from other pigs – that can then be transferred to its home environment. Do not let your pig eat or drink from others food and water bowls – remember to take your own. As soon as you get home, clean and disinfect the bowls and clean and change the bedding your pig has used whilst outside of the home environment.

2) Breed Standards - American Pot-bellied Pig Standard

Unlike normal sized pig breeds or hogs, pot-bellied pigs cannot participate in official contests such as hog shows or swine shows because they are developed solely as a pet companion and therefore cannot qualify for hog standards. However, you can still show off your pot-bellied pigs by participating in several costume or designer shows where owners get to dress up their pets. Although these shows mainly judge your pot-bellied pig's dress, sometimes they may also include the pot-bellied pig breed standard and the tricks it can do in the criteria for judging. Below is the standard size for an American Pot-bellied Pig.

Body Size and Condition:
Measures about 15 – 20 inches from the top of the shoulders at 5 years old.
Overall weight may vary but it should be proportionate with its stature.
The pot-bellied pig should have no mobility issues and should be able to run and move freely with no support.

Head:
The head of your pot-bellied pig should be proportionate to its body. The eyes should not be obstructed, they must be open and should have clear vision; there should be no eye discharge.
The teeth and mouth should have no defects; it must be clean, proportional and free from dental or mouth diseases.

The forehead slopes to its snout; length may vary but it should be proportional.

Ears
Should be erect.
Must be relatively small and proportional.

Neck
Must have no excessive jowls or should not have a fatty neck.
Must be proportionate to its body.

Body
The pot-bellied pig's body should be proportional, compact and well balanced. Preferably has a strong and athletic appearance.

Back
The pot-bellied pig's back should be vertical or straight without a prominent sway.

Tail
Its tail should be natural and straight.
It should have a tassel at the end.

Feet and Legs
The legs should be proportionate, straight and must look strong and appealing. The toes in its hooves should be even and facing forward.

Hair
The pot-bellied pig's hair should be healthy and coarse.
Its length and thickness should adapt with the season.

Color
American pot-bellied pigs have a wide variety of colors and patterns (color/pattern requirements may vary from one contest to another).

Sex Characteristics
Males should have two proportional, palpable testicles set in the scrotum. Female mammary glands should at least have 12 inch space between them.

Temperament
Pot-bellied pigs should be friendly and intelligent, with an even or calm temperament, and be able to do tricks.

Disqualification
If a pot-bellied pig suffers from illnesses and abnormalities such as hernia, mule foot, heavy wrinkling, swayed back, wattles, etc. they will be disqualified.

Important Note
Pot-bellied pigs breed and qualification standards may vary in one contest to another. The guidelines provided in this section are only based on the American Pot-bellied Pig Association. The pot-bellied pig standard can also be used as a guide when purchasing or choosing a pot-bellied pig from a breeding stock.

Chapter 11. Pet Insurance

1) What To Look For In A Pet Insurance Plan

Like medical costs for humans, hospitalization and veterinary bills for pet animals can rack up quite a large a sum. This is why companies have started to offer pet insurance coverage for those who wish to avoid the headache of discovering how much it costs when your pet has a disease or illness. You may have to pay an excess on the cost of treatment, but insurance does give you the peace of mind, for a monthly fee, of being able to afford to get your pet pig treatment by a professional when required.

With more and more people discovering the joy of having pets at home, companies who are offering pet insurance have tripled in recent years. There are plenty of options out there for you to choose from that will offer you the perfect package in order to meet the needs of your pet pig.

However, too many options can also be problematic, particularly if you are new to the pet insurance world. I must stress, however, that it is totally worthwhile to invest in a pet plan that is right for you, as you never know when extra costs may arise. Go online and compare a few websites, speak to other owners of pet pigs, get in touch with breeders or speak to your vet. These are all good sources for advice. Here are some things to look for when considering which plan to go for.

1. Duration Period Length

This is perhaps the number one priority when choosing your plan. You need to look for a lifetime plan rather than a plan that you must renew every 12 months. If you choose a lifetime plan, you do not have to go through the hassle of renewing or possibly changing plans every year. Imagine what would happen if you forgot to renew it one year; the costs could be extreme for you, and you pet as well in terms of stress and waiting lists. Of course, annual plans are cheaper, but lifetime policies are much safer to go for in the event of an unexpected accident or illness.

2. Coverage Protection

Another important aspect to consider if what is actually covered under the policy. Some policies will only cover medical bills after they have gotten sick, whereas others will also include preventive care. Preventive care can be vaccinations, for example.

Conclusion

I hope you have found the information contained in this book to be useful, if you are either already a proud owner of a pet pot-bellied pig, or are considering getting one.

As with any pet, it is a huge commitment and responsibility – not to mention an expense – but also, as with any pet, the joy that owning your own pet pot-bellied pig can bring is immeasurable.

I have never regretted a single day since I became a pot belly pig owner. Each day brings adventures as she learns and shows off her tricks, expresses her range of piggy emotions through her personality and brings delight to everyone in the family – including our other pets. She has become, as with all the animals in our life, simply another member of the family!

I wish you all good luck and happiness on your piggy journey!

CPSIA information can be obtained
at www.ICGtesting.com
Printed in the USA
LVOW10s1816031117
554902LV00010B/736/P

9 781788 650007